LIFE
OVERCOMER

DAPHNE LEIGH

WESTBOW
PRESS®
A DIVISION OF THOMAS NELSON
& ZONDERVAN

Scripture taken from the King James Version of the Bible.

WestBow Press books may be ordered through
booksellers or by contacting:

WestBow Press
A Division of Thomas Nelson & Zondervan
1663 Liberty Drive
Bloomington, IN 47403
www.westbowpress.com
1 (866) 928-1240

ISBN: 978-1-9736-1413-5 (sc)
ISBN: 978-1-9736-1412-8 (e)

Print information available on the last page.

WestBow Press rev. date: 01/19/2018

Contents

ACKNOWLEDGEMENTS

I want to thank those people in my life for their constant support as I work on this book. Mom, Dad, Sisters and Brothers, your influence in my life has helped to shape me into the person I am today. Christian Family, your support and prayers have watched me grow from my first wobbly steps as a new Christian at age 21, and have helped me through each experience in life. You have never shied away from speaking hard truths to me and for that I am thankful.

My group of editors from my Home Group consists mostly of retired school teachers. Gang, this mission would be mission impossible without your help and support.

And for all the others God brings along the way, thank you, thank you and God bless you. It does take a village of committed, faith filled people to complete a project like this. May God bless it and help it to encourage others.

INTRODUCTION

Wouldn't it be wonderful if life were perfect? I remember as a child I loved to listen to fairy tales, where everyone's dreams come true. Just at the perfect moment, the Fairy God Mother arrived on the scene, gave the poor underprivileged hero or heroine of the fairy tale just the courage, grace, or strength they needed, and changed a hurtful situation into something beautiful. And they all lived happily ever after. This is the perfect fantasy that our children are encouraged to believe. But what happens when life isn't exactly perfect, when the problems in a person's life are so overwhelming that they can hardly see it through to the next day? I'm afraid this situation needs more than a quick fix brought by the magical fairy god mother. In the situations and pain of my life, I have found the answer is in a personal and vital relationship with God through his Son, Jesus Christ. He is the one who can make the pain of life make sense, and through the pain allow us to learn about ourselves and how we relate to others. Then the healing process can start.

It is my hope and prayer through this book that many might see the love of God, and find hope through whatever they may be going through. Maybe my story can touch a life or encourage some struggling person to keep trying and never give up. I endeavor to give hope to all who read this book, that God is more than able to speak to any situation and shed light on either the way out or the way to overcome it. Sometimes through persistence and "hanging tough" we become stronger, wiser, more patient and truly can become a "LIFE OVERCOMER".

At the very back of this book I will include a prayer that will lead any person interested into a personal, vital relationship with God through his only Son, Jesus. This prayer can begin to unleash God's power to heal and deliver you as His child from situations that seem too hard to handle. By continuing on in fellowship with Him and with His people you will be led into a new and exciting journey of life. It will be the best decision you have ever made for now, and eternity.

CHAPTER ONE

Life Overcomer

Many people have great memories of being a child. Sure there are times when all kids are made fun of, or when challenges seem too great, and the emotional turmoil that comes with growing up seems too much. This is normal, and time heals all wounds. My life memories of being very young are not so great. I mostly remember pain. Many people who are born with special challenges can understand what that pain feels like. My challenges reached from physical to learning challenges to weigh control to emotional problems. I believe I was a person who was born without basic survival abilities, and left in the world to learn how to survive.

Sometimes problems start in creation. I was born with a slight birth defect n my legs, where my knee caps were smaller than they should have been. This led to physical problems growing up which caused great pain and emotional stress, as I will get into later in this chapter. I also believe the learning difficulties were something I was born with. As a young child, I was colicky and sick for a time, which did damage to my thyroid gland, contributing to a weight problem which started at a young age. These challenges had a great impact on my self esteem. And the self esteem problems followed me into my adult years. I am still replacing those old messages and messages of failure with messages of "Newness in Christ" even after 25 years of following the Lord. The truth is, healing is a process. But, there is always a light at the end of the tunnel.

I appreciate so much the parents that God gave me, and all they did to try to hold my hand through the challenges I faced, and still am facing. My prayer is that they, too, will come to relationship with Christ, and find the healing that He provides for the hurts of this life.

I was raised in an upper class neighborhood in Seattle, Washington. I really had the best of everything. But even the best of families have challenges, and we had ours. My parents have stayed together through 55 years of marriage, through the good times and the bad. They loved us, and each other enough to get help when they needed it, and to try to help us deal with whatever we went through growing up. I was in 2nd grade when my school teachers started wondering if I had some learning problems. I went to a small private school for Kindergarten and 1st grade, and didn't advance much in learning there. As I entered into the public school system and began to learn how to read and write I tried to learn the basics. I really struggled with just the simplest things. One problem I had was proportions. I couldn't seem to write my letters or numbers the same size. I also had challenges with writing letters and numbers backwards.

I remember learning to write cursive, and slanting my letters one way, and changing in the middle of the word and slanting the other way. For someone with learning disabilities it was nearly impossible to write a term paper, a letter, or even a sentence without making a mistake. (You must remember, these were the days before Bill Gates & personal computers.) I would try again and again. Always in the first paragraph of what I was writing I would leave out key words, or spell a word incorrectly, and have to start all over again. At last I would give up and have to turn in a flawed paper. I also had attention span problems. It seemed that I just wasn't aware of all that was happening around me, my brain wasn't able to process all the information.

Also by the time I was school age, I was already starting to battle with a weight problem. As most of you know, Kids can be brutal to each other. I was constantly being seen as the overweight child, or the class air head. This can do a real number on the self esteem of any child, especially one who has two older sisters who were both high achievers. My grades through school were somewhere around C average. Music was always my saving grace, and any time I was in music class my grades were a little higher.

I also endured a lot of bullying from someone which continued into adulthood. This person was older than me, smarter than me (as she did not have my learning disabilities), naturally gifted, but very unhappy. They decided that the way to make themself happy was to make me (and sometimes others) feel worse than they did. Anything I tried they could pick up and in a day or two was way ahead of me. This reinforced the self esteem issues I was already having and made me feel ashamed. It took many years after adulthood (and Christ in my life) to distinguish the truth from a lie, and let the Word of God shape who I was to become and how I felt about myself. There has been much talk in the news lately about bullying. I heard a report this week addressing bulling at home, saying that it is as harmful as bullying outside the home. What a news flash! If you are raising kids, please take this issue seriously. If you suspect bullying in your home, or if you child talks to you about what is going on please address it and take care if it to the best of your ability. The outside world is harsh enough for kids. Home needs to be a refuge.

I was tested for learning disabilities and dyslexia twice as a child, and both tests came back negative. Even today I can't explain why. I know the struggle I was going through just getting the basics down in grade school. I believe that one reason is that back in the 1960's, when the testing took place not that much was known about learning styles. I honestly think that God had a plan for me, to change and mold me into His image, and that would not have happened if I had not gone through some of the years of hurtful lessons I had to go through on my own.

Things started to change for me physically at about age 9. I remember playing ball with my brother in the basement of our home, and falling really hard on one knee as I went after the ball. He helped me over to the stairwell and I sat there for a while until the pain subsided, and I thought I was well again. And it was, for about the next week. What actually happened is that when I fell I had stretched out the ligament in my left knee. That along with the slight birth defect of knee caps that were too small for the rest of my bone structure led to my greatest childhood nightmare.

It started one evening when I was getting ready for bed. My parents were out to a special dinner, one of those rare dates that parents have when they have four children! My sister, then 12 years of age was watching us, making sure we behaved. Well as I got ready for bed, something happened to my left leg. I didn't know what it was, all I knew was that I was in the worst pain I'd ever been in. I collapsed on the floor of my bedroom, screaming at the top of my lungs. My sisters and brother all came running to find out what was wrong, and no one knew what to do. We were all terrorized by what had happened to me. Well, Sis went to call my parents at the restaurant, and when they arrived home, my Dad picked me up off the floor and carried me to the car to take me to Emergency. I remember as my Mother backed the car out of the carport, something happened again, and the pain went away. I rested in the arms of my father, and knew that it was all right again. I remember that moment today as one of the best memories of my childhood. My Dad was there taking care of me, the pain was gone, and I knew my parents loved me. What we found out at the hospital was that the stretched out ligament had allowed my left knee to go completely out of joint, the knee cap moving to the left, to the outside of my leg. What had happened when my Mom was backing the car out of the driveway, is that my knee cap had snapped back into place, so subsiding the pain.

We left the hospital that night with an ace bandage, and a rented pair of crutches. I'm sure the doctors felt this would be a one time incident, and there was nothing to worry about. That, however, is not how the situation worked out.

CHAPTER TWO

Living the Nightmare

I had it all going for me. A great family (aside from normal sibling rivalry), great parents who stayed together through thick and thin, a beautiful country club type neighborhood, great school, the best of everything in life. But sometimes these "things" can't even begin to meet emotional needs of hurting children, or answer those tough questions that come up in life.

After my first incident with the knee problem, the dislocations became more and more frequent. Before long, the ligaments had been stretched out so drastically, that it took next to nothing to throw that knee out of joint. I would just be walking down the sidewalk (usually all alone) step on one of those cracks in the sidewalk, or on a little pebble that would make my foot turn slightly, and I would be on the cement in extreme pain, with a dislocated knee cap. I'm sure it was one of those lovely incidents that helped to stretch out the ligaments in the other knee, and what I ended up with was two dislocating knee caps. My parents did all they could for me. They sent me to the best bone specialists in the city to try and correct the problem. The doctors felt it would be best to wait until I had reached my full height potential, at age 15 or 16, and then to operate.

So the rented crutches were exchanged for my very own pair, which sat dutifully in my bedroom closet when I didn't need them. Those poor doctors tried everything: Leg splints, casts, taping my knees to keep them in joint, nothing helped. So they taught me to fix the problem – how to put a dislocated knee back into place. All I had to do was to take the leg, straighten it out and as I did, grasp the knee cap with both hands and pop it back into place. That is – after I recovered from the temporary trauma that always hit the moment it happened. Easier said than done, but I learned how to do it. I had to. The physical problem got so bad that I could be doing just simple things like turning over in my bed at night, and I would start to feel that knee dislocate. More trauma, more pain. There were no answers but to wait 6 or 7 years for surgery.

One time I was walking around in our back yard. I was alone, as I usually was when it happened. I was just hanging out trying to be a normal kid. I guess I stepped on an uneven place on the lawn. There it went, my knee popped to the outside of my leg. More trauma. I laid on the lawn for a few moments to recover my nerves. Then I had to fix it. So I slowly stretched out my leg, grasped my knee with both my hands and popped it back in place. After I sat there for another five minutes until the throbbing started to subside, I drug myself back up the stairs and in the house. "Mom, it happened again" I announced as I hobbled inside. She ran for the ace bandages, out came the crutches and I would be back on both feet in three or four days until it happened again.

Another time I was at the wonderful summer camp we went to every summer. This place was such a refuge to me. Even though I couldn't hike as fast or as well as the other kids (they used to call me inch-an-hour....it was kind of funny) I could swim in the pool and the creek, ride horses, have wonderful campfires, enjoy music, and make special friends I could see again every summer. One afternoon I was trying to play volleyball with a group of other kids. My oldest sister was there with me. As I went for the ball, there it happened again. As I fell to the ground in pain, the group of kids gathered around me, staring at me. My sister knelt by my side, holding my hand as I dealt with the trauma. She said my lips turned blue from the pain. After a few minutes I could move again, and said "Ok, you guys, I have to fix this now". So I slowly stretched out my leg and popped my knee back in place amidst shouts of "GROSS!!" The camp director called my parents in Seattle, then they took me to a doctor in Granite Falls near the camp. The doctor taped my leg, put me in a cast and sent me back to camp. My parents offered to take me back home, but I chose to stay at the camp. Just another survival story.

I remember another incident that involved another sister. She is two years older than I am, and my fiercest rival and competitor growing up. But she also could be my greatest advocate. Of course as a young girl, a sister without my learning and physical handicaps was a pretty hard act to follow, but I refused to let her get the best of me. There was one week when I was in fourth grade and I was spending another week on crutches after a lovely episode with my knee problems. There was an older neighborhood boy who was constantly picking on me and bullying me. I was standing in the lunch line at school with my sister right behind me. This boy walked past me and said "Hey, what happened? Did you break your head?" The comment angered my sister so much that she walked up to me and grabbed one of my crutches and applied it firmly to one of his shins. Then she turned back to me, gave me my crutch back, and got back into the lunch line. The poor boy – with the force of my sister's arm, he probably received a permanent dent in that leg. Funny thing – I don't remember him bullying me again after that.

The only way to describe what constant fear the physical problem put me in is to think of the movie Jaws. The shark is there. You are on a raft, floating in the ocean. The shark knows where you are, and you can't get out of the water. The shark will attack. It's just a matter of time. That fear became so prevalent in my life growing up it literally became part of my personality. And in many ways I acted out that fear in dysfunctional behavior. I won't go into any details, but I had some very strange habits, that other kids thought were very un-cool.

The weight problems continued as I approached Junior High. The combination of the physical problem and the low thyroid didn't help the situation. To make matters worse, I had learned how to use food as a tool to deal with the fears and emotional problems that were developing. I entered Weight Watchers in the Seventh Grade along with a neighbor girl, and we both reached lifetime membership. But the problems that put the weight on weren't dealt with, so the struggle continued into adulthood.

As I advanced in school the learning problems continued, and my self confidence in learning went lower and lower. It didn't help that I had two older sisters who excelled in school and got A's on their report cards all the time. The experts told my parents that I was a bright girl and I could learn if I applied myself. There were no answers to what I was struggling with when learning to write a paper, do math, even speaking. My words would not come out right, and the other kids thought it was pretty funny. Writing a paper was extremely difficult as I couldn't write even a few sentences without making a mistake. Learning to spell was nearly impossible. I might spell a word right one time, and miss it in the next sentence. Reading was a challenge, because I felt like entire blocks of information were not registering. It was like I had a blind spot and couldn't see the whole page. I was accused time and time again of not applying myself. All I can say is that you can run into a brick wall only so many times, and then you start to avoid the brick wall.

I know that I was a frustration to my teachers, and my parents did what they could to help. They probably helped me more than they should have in getting my homework correct. The truth always came out on the tests I took. I remember struggling to learn to add, multiply and divide, sitting for hours with my father trying to get the equations straight in my mind. My father would catch me making a mistake, and I would just stare at the equation, and wonder "What did I do wrong?". They tried to arrange tutors a few times in grade school but it really didn't help much. I think I was a bit of a frustration to them too.

In the fifth grade I started to play the violin. (My sisters both played beautifully, so I had to learn how to play it too.) Well, the grade school band instructor sat me down when he heard that I wanted to play with the school orchestra. He explained to me that I would have to work very hard and do the best job I could to play with the other children. I agreed wholeheartedly to try my hardest if he would let me play. The poor man! I was the little girl in the back of the orchestra whose bow was continually going the opposite direction of the other violin players. He knew how talented my sisters were. I'm sure he was wondering what happened with me! My biggest challenge musically was that because of the learning challenges I could not learn how to read music. All the notes looked the same. So I learned to have an ear for what the notes were supposed to sound like, and mimicked what I heard. Also, being naturally dyslexic, my natural tendency was to do things backwards, which explains the theory of the violin bow going the wrong direction. But music was in my soul, and by age 10 I had also picked up the guitar, the instrument I stayed with and excelled in. I stayed with the violin though the seventh grade and took some private lessons. (I think I frustrated the violin teacher too!) I was second violin, last chair in the Junior High orchestra. The next year I gave it up to focus my energy on guitar and singing. So ended my career as a violinist.

I remember an incident in the sixth grade with a teacher I really loved and admired. There were some special projects I was trying to do with my science class, and I was struggling with them as usual. I was out at recess, playing with the other kids. This teacher found me on the playground and pulled me aside, and said to me "I just wanted to warn you that you are flunking science". Not: "Let's stay late together after class and work on this", not "Let's get you some help", just "I just wanted you to know that you are flunking science." Now this was not a bad teacher. This was a very good teacher who didn't understand my learning challenges. I know she was comparing me to my Sisters and my Brother, and wondering why I couldn't learn and they could. Most teachers probably thought that I didn't care, or that I just wasn't concentrating hard enough or taking my studies seriously enough. I think most of it was the "brick wall" syndrome. Even when I gave it my best shot, it just wasn't good enough.

By the time I reached Junior High School I started to withdraw emotionally. The physical and learning problems were getting to be more than I could handle, and no one could help me. There were no answers for my life. What I needed was a perfect little world where no one could hurt me, make fun of me, or laugh at me. Where there was no pain, no more tears. So I created this perfect world in my own mind, and I escaped there whenever I was overwhelmed by all that was happening in my life. The more time went on, the more I escaped into my own mind. You see, life to me was like a giant asphalt roller that the road crews use to work on our roads. The giant asphalt roller would roll over me, and flatten me. Then when I recovered from that episode I would start to get back up on my feet and put myself back together, again would come the giant asphalt roller and flatten me. When I recovered from the shock of this one, I would shake myself, get back up and try again.. The older I got, the more the asphalt roller squashed me, the more I withdrew. In my mind, I became someone else in another place, with the abilities and accomplishments I wanted to have in my own life. I remember seeing a play as a teenager about a man who created his own little country in his own mind. And in that country he became the President. He was very successful and very powerful. When given the choice to join the real world and get married and raise a family, or stay in the imaginary world where everything was perfect, he chose that imaginary world. I identified with the man in that play.

The transition into Junior High was not a real easy one. The classes were harder, the pressure to learn intensified. Again, music was my salvation. I had some great choir instructors in Junior High and High School who really believed in me, and in my abilities. They did a lot to encourage me. Also the music courses I took helped me keep my grades a little higher. There were the teachers that were so domineering that they made a point to embarrass the "slower students" in front of the others. But there were also other teachers who understood what most teens go through, and were really great. My goal at that time was to survive until the physical problem could be corrected. And hopefully somehow I could learn how to understand my text books, and write papers without making mistakes in spelling, grammar, punctuation, or leaving words out of sentences. At least if I couldn't do these things in the real world, I could in my world.

CHAPTER THREE

Freedom at Last

'Ninth Grade was a big year for me. I remember visiting my favorite knee doctor that summer before school started, and he decided that I was finally old enough and tall enough to go through the surgery to fix my knee problems. I just stared back at him in disbelief. I had finally arrived. My parents scheduled my first knee surgery for that September. I was a little nervous going into it but very anxious to get it over with. In the hospital after the surgery I remember being on major pain killers and in major pain. There were fun times too of racing down the halls of the hospital in a wheelchair with another girl my age. (Those poor nurses!) I spent a few weeks at home recuperating after each operation, and ended up missing quite a lot of School. But I was free. I knew that my knees would never dislocate again. It was such a relief to finally be able to go on with the rest of my life and have that worry behind me. Going back to School on crutches and in a full leg brace I was thankful that the stairs I needed to conquer had wider and smaller steps. I wore blue jeans with the leg slit all the way up to my thigh, revealing my very stylish leg splint.

My friend and neighbor was a Christian girl and she had been praying for me. Soon after my second surgery she invited me to a Campus Life meeting. Campus Life is a Christian group of young people who meet weekly to fellowship and study scripture together. I agreed to go, and as I walked into the group meeting, I got a surprise. I saw a man at the front of the group wearing a full leg cast on his left leg. I looked down at my leg, comparing his cast to the splint I had on my leg. There was an immediate connection between us. He pointed to me, to my leg, and then to his leg and we both started to laugh. It's like we said in our minds "I know what happened to me...what happened to you?" The man was the Northwest Director of Campus Life at that time. Apparently he had gone out onto his porch to retrieve a newspaper, slipped on some ice and fallen, breaking his leg. As he had already gotten my attention I thought maybe I should listen to what the man had to say. I heard the Gospel of Jesus Christ for the first time in my life. He shared the scripture John 3:16– "For God so loved the world that he gave his only begotten Son that whosoever believeth on Him should not perish, but have everlasting life." I was impressed with his message. After the meeting we got together and shared war stories about our legs, and he encouraged me to pray with him to accept Christ. All I know is that I had gone through enough of this life on my own. I knew that I needed God's help to handle the problems I was facing. I really believe that God had allowed this guy to have an accident and break his leg because the Lord knew that I would show up and we would have that connection. I will always be thankful for these good people for showing me the way to Christ. Going home to my family that evening I faced a challenge that I never imagined. I was so excited about my new commitment to Jesus that the first thing I did when I hobbled in the door is announce that I had given my heart to Jesus and become a Christian. This news, I'm sure, came as quite a shock to my family. It led to a lot of (normal) heckling from my brother and sisters, and concern from my parents as well, as I was only 15 years old. I'm sure they felt I was too young to make such a decision. But, thankfully, they allowed me to attend the Campus Life meetings regularly.

My neighbor invited me to go to the Presbyterian church with her and to their youth gatherings when I could, but it didn't mean as much to me as the Campus Life connection. The Campus Life director had became a friend and a father to me. I continued to attend these meetings into high school until he was called to help in the healing of a church in California and take over the pastorate there. The young people I met at the Campus Life meetings became my close friends, and helped me stay out of trouble in High School. They did a lot to mentor me as I tried to follow Christ without the support of a local church.

The fifteenth year of my life was the best year yet. Even with the pain of surgeries and recovery, it brought me a double freedom – physical and spiritual. I acquired a great love for God, even though I didn't understand the Word of God very well, or his love for me. I still had so many questions, trying to make sense of my life.

It seemed like my classmates, even the ministers I talked to, and asked these tough questions never had enough of the answers.

I did eventually drift from the faith for a while after my Campus Life director left for California. The Campus Life club was replaced by Young Life in High School, and that wasn't my crowd. I felt like I didn't belong with them.. But God is faithful, and when my time was right I did receive all the strength and faith I needed to make that firm commitment to Him. I really believe I had no clue about what issues I was dealing with emotionally, or the battle that was being waged for my soul. I needed power and strength to fight that battle to win and I couldn't do that without the support of a local church and the power of His Holy Spirit. That came later.

Even though both my legs were "fixed" in the ninth grade, the emotional struggle continued. I continually had flashbacks in my mind of my knees dislocating and those flashbacks would simply paralyze me. When I recovered from the memory again, I would tell myself "You're OK. That will never happen to you again." School was still extremely difficult and again I took refuge in music. Those music grades helped me to keep my GPA at a 2.75. I dreaded history, geography and current event classes. I actually did ok in English (surprisingly) and I remember only taking one math class in High School which I barely passed. I took horticulture to get out of taking biology. My sixth grade science episode made me shy away from taking biology. Again there were some teachers that were very domineering, very embarrassing to me, and some who were wonderful.

CHAPTER FOUR

Trying to Survive in a Big World

One of my nightmares was learning how to drive. Being naturally dyslexic, I have problems sometimes telling my right from my left. So during driver's education I would many times signal the wrong way when trying to make a turn. The instructor was one of those types who made me very nervous. You know – the kind that loves to point out all your errors, and finds humor in them. My mom also expressed frustration when driving around with me, observing that I just wasn't aware of what was happening around me. At first my friends were afraid to ride with me because it took me so long to catch on to the rules of the road. That first semester of driver's education I flunked, because the instructor thought I was too nervous behind the wheel – sure I was, with him in the car! Well, I just kept practicing, and eventually went with an independent instructor who was wonderful, and had a very gentle spirit. I passed the course with no problem, and went on to get my license. After catching on through experience to some of my learning difficulties and how it affected my driving, I went on to be an excellent, very defensive driver. I learned that because my eyes have very little depth perception not to take any chances when turning into traffic or pulling onto the highway. I just can't trust myself in those situations. Eventually I won back the confidence of those friends who had been nervous driving with me, and life went on.

What was very scary looking back now, is that as I got older I was spending more and more time in that private world in my mind. Reality was just too difficult. I would enter into that world every night before I went to sleep and many mornings I would awaken still in that world. I realize now that this was actually a form of mental illness. And no one knew about it but me. I never talked about it. I was like a walking time bomb ready to fall apart. High School was full of very harmful influences. There were drugs, alcohol, cigarettes all around me. When I think about what the other kids, even some close friends and family members were involved in, it makes me shudder. But these things weren't really a temptation to me. I had no interest in drugs. Being around the cigarettes and pot made me physically ill. When it came to drinking, even as an adult I could only take one or two sips, and I'd had enough. I really believe the evidence of God's hand on my life was the reason for this. The commitment I made to Christ at 15 gave me a love for God, and that love for God kept me safe.

What I really longed for was a warm, fuzzy world where there was security and happiness and love. The only world like that I knew was in my mind. I believe that the one area I could have gone overboard in my life is that of relationships. There is a philosophy in modern psychology that if there is not a strong love bond between fathers and their daughters, the daughters will end up looking for that love somewhere else. It's not that I didn't love and respect my Father. In my own way I really did. But I also saw first hand the struggles in my parent's marriage. I am so thankful that they cared enough for each other, and for their children to stay together through that struggle. I also believe that in many ways, the four of us children were affected by that struggle. I was the youngest of the four. During that formative time of ages 12 − 18 my father was dealing very seriously with his own issues in life, and working to make it better. He was also working very hard to make a struggling business succeed. I guess there wasn't a whole lot of time left over for me. This did create some resentment, and a real hunger for love and attention in my heart. Since my dad wasn't always available, I looked for other male attention. This was part of my "perfect world" mentality. I am so thankful today for God's hedge of protection over me during that time. Weight problems didn't make me real attractive back then. But the guys I couldn't get in real life could be mine in my private world. Everything was perfect there − I had the love, acceptance and success I needed to make it in life. It took quite a while after total commitment to Christ to break through to that perfect world. Deception had become a way of life, and I kind of liked it. Reality didn't compute for me. There was just too much pain.

One thing I can say now is that my dad and I have both done a lot of growing since then, and have really come to appreciate each other. There has been a real healing in our relationship and now he is one of my best friends. If there are relationship challenges in your family, I encourage you to work hard at making things better. I did, and I'm glad I did. It only takes one person to start the process of healing. And after you start working at it, don't give up. It takes time and lots of hard work to really make things better.

As a high school student I was welcomed into my parents business to work part time while I finished school. This was great work experience, but also my first taste of what it's like to hold down a job when you have learning disabilities. And I thought school was tough! Let's just say that the margin of error was very high and my parents did everything they could to encourage me and make it easier. I remember one time mailing out premium gifts to new customers and forgetting to put the address labels on the gifts! I did become a pretty good file clerk though. It really helped in finalizing my memorizing of the alphabet! I did little tasks for one of the clerks, Leone, who became a good friend. I also helped with some of their bulk mailings and billings.

At last I did reach graduation from high school. I took 5 weeks off right after graduation to tour Europe with People to People which was a real blessing. I made some good friends and learned a lot about other cultures. When I returned home again my friends from high school went off to college and I went to work for my parents. Personally, I'd had enough of school for a while.

So I worked for my parents for my first 6 years after high school. That was definitely one of the loneliest times of my life. My school friends were away at college, my brother and sisters were mostly gone and getting on with their own lives. It was just me, my parents, my dog and my guitar. My dog and my guitar ranked pretty high on that list of friends back then. I really enjoyed working with the young girls my parents had hired to work in the office, but the truth is that I was the bosses' daughter and after hours they didn't really include me in much of their activities. So I spent time with my parents, my dog and my guitar and existed in my own little private world. I was starting to learn to act out some of the fantasies I was having in my mind and again, the hand of The Lord came in to rescue me and hedge me in with his protection. I was putting myself in situations where anything could have happened to me, my heart was so starved for the wrong kind of attention. One time I was sitting outside on a bluff a few blocks from home, all alone, playing my guitar and singing. There was a man parked there who was a total stranger listening to the music. Now that I think of it, he really wasn't a safe looking kind of guy. There had been reports of young girls being attacked previously just up the street from there. Well, my father happened to drive by and saw me. He insisted that I get in the car and go home with him. Even though I rebelled from that inside, I listened to him and got in the car. Thank God I did. I can't tell how many times I almost put myself in a situation that would have been very harmful, but a parent or a friend stepped in and said "No, you will not do this!" and saved my hide.

My real dream back then was to take my music into the night clubs and bars of Seattle, as my step brother had done, and to become good enough to really entertain people there. I know now the pitfalls that come with that lifestyle. I am so thankful that God rescued me in time before I had a chance to really ruin things forever. I know the slippery slope I was heading down even if no one else could see it. Sometimes it is the ones who are only inwardly destructive, and the actions or motives are unseen to the outside world, who are in the most danger.

On my 21st birthday, my desire was to go out with close friends (which I did not have) and go bar hopping. That would have signified that I had really arrived socially. But there were no friends, no invitations. Instead I had a quiet family party with my parents and grandparents. I was devastated! (You can see where I was heading. I should have been thankful to be surrounded by loving family members!) I had just come home from my first attempt at college, enrolling at Washington State University in Pullman, Washington. Another one of my dreams, being a country girl at heart, was to get away from the big city and study to be a veterinarian. It was so exiting to move into the dorm, meet new friends and finally be in a beautiful country setting. But academically I didn't know what I was up against. I still struggled with basic English and Spelling. I had never learned how to write a paper properly and was still blocking out entire sections of paragraphs when I read or studied. Needless to say, my career as a student at Washington State didn't last long. I couldn't even make it one quarter.

I had a great love for music and drama and ended up

taking two drama courses. One of them was evaluating dramatic literature. On my first test I thought I had done pretty well. I had really studied and was so proud of myself for working so hard. But when I took the test I didn't realize that I needed to turn the test page over, and complete the back of the page (Duh!). When I returned to class the next day I found out that I had failed the test. My first attempt to write a college paper didn't go much better. I was so excited to try, and really did my best, but remember back then there were no personal computers with spell check. Using a dictionary was foreign to me. And don't ask someone with dyslexia to find their own mistakes when they are writing or typing something. They'll miss most of them. After I turned that paper in that I was so very proud of, the professor made a pretty thorough example of it, on how not to write a paper. In fact, it was the class's biggest joke of the day. Again, there was no help in how to do it right, just an example of how not to do it. I'll give the man a little credit – he did come up to me after class and say "I hope that didn't hurt too much". He still had a grin on his face, though. I could tell he was still very amused. I ended up packing my things that weekend, and coming back home to Seattle. It was years before I tried the big University experience again. A word to the wise for teachers. Please try and be gracious when dealing with struggling students. They don't need your harassment, they need your help. Not all students learn at the same level. It would have meant so much more for someone to take me by the hand and show me how to write, instead of just laughing at me. I am so thankful that more is being done now about learning styles, and teaching instructors different methods to reach different children. I believe this would have made a great difference for me.

So I headed home in total defeat to rejoin the team at my parents' office. It was pretty embarrassing, as I was expecting to stay in Eastern Washington and not return home for quite a few years. But that defeat lead to the experience that really changed my life.

CHAPTER FIVE

New Life

Sometimes people really need to hit bottom before they can look up and ask for help. I remember during my nineteenth and twentieth years I kept telling myself and other people that I needed to find a good church, get involved with its people and its programs, and get my life straightened out. Some people I talked to laughed at that idea, telling me that churches have problems too, and that they were full of hypocrites anyhow. But my previous commitment to Christ and my own heart told me differently. I just didn't know how to get started.

At age 20 I had an experience with the Lord that really blew me away, showing the steadfastness and forgiveness of God even when I wasn't even following him. I loved him, but was locked into my own habits and lost in my sin. Well, the dog that our family had since I was 10 years old had a stroke and was dying. I remember sitting beside Lucky on our basement floor and watching her slow, labored breathing, wondering if each breath would be her last. My parents were upstairs preparing to take her to the vet and I could hear them crying up there. I knew enough about the Word of God to know that the Jesus of the Bible healed people. I felt so inadequate to ask the Lord for anything, but I didn't want to lose my puppy. So I prayed to Jesus. "Lord Jesus, if you will touch my dog and heal her, I promise that when it is really her time to die that I will be willing to let her go. But please right now, touch my dog and make her better. Amen." By the time I was done praying my parents were ready to take her to the vet. She was paralyzed by the stroke, so they had to pick her up and carry her to the car. As they drove off I went to my bedroom, dusted off my Bible, and started to read it, all the time wondering what would happen. When they returned from the vet they had a very amazing story to tell. Apparently, by the time they had gotten to the vet's office (about 5 minutes from our house), Lucky was able to lift her head. By the time they got her inside she was standing up on the examination table. After the vet examined her they really couldn't find much wrong with her. So they just decided to keep her overnight for observation and we could take her home the next day. That's when my tears really started. I knew that I was not in the right place to ask God for anything but His grace overrode my lifestyle. And, by the way, when my dog finally did die, one year later, I was safely in the Kingdom of God, filled with His Spirit and able to let her go.

During my short time at Washington State University I started thinking that maybe Business School would be a better idea for me, getting specific training to enter a career. So when I returned home in November of 1977 I started looking into different schools. I worked for

my parents until March of 1978 and then entered ITT
Peterson School of Business. It was definitely easier for
me and I really enjoyed the students who went there. I
felt like I had finally found something that would make
my life work for a while. During my first quarter there
I met Sylvia. She was a Christian girl, recently filled
with the Holy Spirit, and very excited about her new life
in Christ and the power that the infilling of the Holy
Spirit had given her. One day I wore my "Campus Life"
t-shirt that I had bought when I was still involved in the
club. She recognized it as a Christian club, and started to
share with me about commitment to Christ. I guess she
figured out that I wasn't really following the lifestyle of a
Christian. The more she shared with me about her church
and her life, the more it reminded me of something out
of the book of Acts. Thank God, I knew enough about
the Bible to know that an experience with the Holy Spirit
was real. When she invited me to spend the weekend with
her and attend church with her on Sunday I accepted her
invitation. Maybe, I thought, this was just what I needed.

During the weekend Sylvia got out her Bible and
started sharing verses in Acts chapter 1 and 2 about the
Holy Spirit, and what it's all about. Acts 1:4-5 says that
God commanded those first disciples, the early church to
"Wait for the promise of the Father, which, he said, you
have heard of me. For John (the Baptist) truly baptized
with water, but you shall be baptized with the Holy Ghost
not many days hence". Acts 1:8 states "But you shall
receive power after the Holy Ghost has come upon you:
and you shall be witnesses unto me both in Jerusalem, and
in Judea, and in Samaria, and unto the uttermost part of

the earth". Acts:2:1-4 goes into detail of how the infilling of the Holy Spirit touched the early church for the first time. "And when the day of Pentecost was fully come, they were all with one accord in one place. And suddenly there came a sound from Heaven as of a rushing mighty wind, and it filled the house where they were sitting. And there appeared unto them cloven tongues like as of fire, and it sat upon each of them. And they were all filled with the Holy Ghost, and began to speak with other tongues as the Spirit gave them utterance" The more that Sylvia shared the more I knew that God was in this, and she agreed to come forward with me on Sunday morning as I recommitted my life to Christ, and asked him to fill me with the Holy Spirit.

The next morning when we walked into her church., I felt the love and acceptance of God instantly. I experienced Christian music like I had never heard before. (Of course, that convinced me even more that I had finally come home.) Then after the morning message, we both went forward together. The Pastor took just a minute to explain about the Holy Spirit, and what it was all about. Then he led me in a prayer of recommitment. When that was done, he and a few others laid their hands on me and started praying for God to fill me with His Holy Spirit. As they prayed for me I started to feel the awesome power of the Lord filling me, and the Lord helped me to speak out in tongues for the first time. I felt like I was releasing a burden I had been carrying for most of my life. Not only did I feel great love from God's people, I literally felt the Love of God all over me, and inside me. The thing that impressed me the most is that I could finally see through all the confusion that had filled my mind concerning commitment to Christ. It all made complete sense to me now. I understood about the family of God, and I knew that I was now one of His family. And I knew that all this was only the beginning for me. After many tears, and hugs, and more tears, I realized that it was now time to go back to life as usual, and I knew that I couldn't do that. I thought of going back to the family environment that met me as a new Christian at age 15 and I panicked. I looked at Sylvia, and said "You've got to help me! I don't want to go back home right now. If I do I'll never survive as a Christian." She talked with her mother for a moment, and came back saying "You can come stay with me and my family for a while, until you get stronger." Relieved, I agreed. Then I thought "How am I going to explain this to my parents"? Well, God had worked that out too. After all I was 21 years old, and old enough to make my own decisions. So I drove my car home and announced as I walked into the house "By the way, I'm going to stay with Sylvia for a while". I went downstairs to my bedroom to start packing my things. I sometimes wonder what my parent's reaction was to this sudden change. I honestly think they knew that I needed some extra help, and were glad that I had found someone who could help me.

It still amazes me how the Lord had totally prepared me for that weekend. He had worked out details of my life to lead up to making it all work out – from the fact that I had done laundry on a different day than usual to have clean clothes to pack, to allowing my parents to release me completely to go with no notice at all. I remember spending the next few months totally overwhelmed by the power and love of God. For the first time of my life I felt totally accepted, loved, and encouraged to go on with my life. Even though the challenges were still great, I knew that I could face them with God's help.

Sylvia and her mother took me to the Bible book store and bought me my first nice bible. And then they took me by the hand and showed me how to live, act, and react in a way that would not hurt myself or others. It was time to start to build the foundation of Christ strong enough to support a stable life. The fullness of the Holy Spirit is a very big part of my testimony, and I know that it took the awesome power of God in my life to really make a difference and to gain victory over the forces that had taken control.

I feel that I need to make a very important point about being baptized in the Holy Spirit. Some well meaning Spirit filled people give the impression that a person will not enter heaven unless they have had this experience. I don't want to become one of those people. I believe that the fullness of the Holy Spirit is available to any Christian who wants it, and that it will lead them to a powerful place in Christ. But I also know that there are thousands of dedicated Christian people in which God has made a life-changing impact on their hearts without the baptism of the Holy Spirit, and I think that is marvelous. We as Christians need to unite under Christ, and fellowship with each other, and not split hairs over doctrine. Doctrinal warfare will only bring division. Relationship with Christ is the one and only way to Heaven, according to the Word of God. John 10:1-5 and verses 7-10 explains this very clearly. "Verily, verily I say unto you, He that enters not by the door into the sheepfold, but climbs in some other way, the same is a thief and a robber. But he that enters in by the door is the shepherd of the sheep. To him the porter opens; and the sheep hear his voice: and he calls his own by name, and leads them out. And when he puts out his own he goes before them, and the sheep follow him: for they know his voice. A stranger they will not follow, but will flee from him: for they don't know the voice of strangers." And verse 7-10 says, "Verily I say unto you, I am the door of the sheep. All that ever came before me are thieves and robbers, but the sheep did not hear them. I am the door; by me if any man enter in, he shall be saved, and shall go in and out and find pasture. The thief comes not but for to steal, and to kill, and to destroy: I am come that they might have life, and that they might have it more abundantly." The chapter goes on to explain the shepherd's explicit love and care for the sheep. Read it for yourself to see the true character of God in Christ Jesus. People, we share a common faith. Let's dwell in harmony together with that belief, and not bring division by pointing out our differences.

I continued attending ITT Peterson Business School, riding the bus with Sylvia while I lived there for about 4 months. I will never be able to repay the her kindness and that of her parents for taking me in and helping me get grounded in the faith. They taught me to pray with the power of God, and taught me how to study the Word of God and really get something out of it. They were God's hand in my life to help with the mission of putting me back together. There were others, too, in those years.

Wonderful pastors and their families took on the challenge of raising me up in the Lord until I could stand on my own two feet. The Christian family was beginning to develop and adopted me in, treating me like a daughter. Most of those relationships are still rock solid today. Even when I did go back to my parents house to live, I almost didn't last in Christ. There were so many attitudes and philosophies in life that I was raised to believe. The word of God somehow didn't line up with those philosophies. I remember one afternoon I had gone to Sylvia's house to pick up some of my things to move back to my parents house. We ended up having a very intense discussion about what we believed, and I think she knew that I was in trouble. In fact I'm sure that when I left her house she got on the telephone and had our circle of friends pray for me, that I would do right by the Lord. I remember driving home thinking about the argument I had with Sylvia, and wondering what to believe. I started thinking in my mind of all that Jesus Christ had done for me in the last few months, and I can tell you the place where I was on the street driving to my parents where I finalized my commitment to Christ. I figured that after all Jesus had done for me, how could I let him down by walking away? I knew then that I wanted to follow Christ with my life. I thank God for those wonderful brothers and sisters in Christ who loved me enough to hang on to me tight and not let me go. What I needed was unconditional love and I found it in God's people.

One of the great battles to be fought with my commitment to Christ was turning my will and my desires over to God, and let him mold and shape them into that new creature in Christ. All my life I had a great love for horses. With my physical problems, riding horses was one thing I could do and I learned to do it very well. During my teen years my sister and I were both allowed to purchase our own horses and we saw them and rode them whenever we could. Those times I had with my horse were like heaven to me. I really loved the country, and the quietness of the places where we boarded them. The challenge of the situation was that living within the city limits of Seattle, we had to drive many miles to visit our horses. I had no car and had to share the car we had with my mother, my sisters and my brother. Needless to say, my visits with my horse were too few and far between. At nineteen I sold my horse and bought my first car. It was then I started investing in riding lessons at a stable in Kirkland, Washington. I already knew pretty much all there was to know about western style riding without getting into rodeo riding and so my interest shifted to hunt seat, and taking the horses over fences. This became a passion for me and my lessons accelerated to twice a week. Of course this hobby became quite expensive and every time I would get to where I was tackling the cross poles in my riding experience I ran out of money and had to stop for a while. By the time I made my commitment to Christ, this was one of the first areas He was asking me to surrender. I knew that the lessons I was taking were during times I should be in church, and I had to make a decision on which direction my life would take. God is a gentleman, and didn't force that decision on me. He let me make my choice. But I knew that choice would have a profound impact on my life. Reluctantly, I laid my passion for horses down at His feet. That passion had become so strong in my life that it was almost like an idol. The word of God says in Exodus 20:3 "You shall have no other gods before me". It's not like I had idols all over my house that I worshiped. But my love for horses was taking up too much of my time and too much of my life. It was limiting what Jesus could do in my heart and life. I needed to give Jesus all of me if I wanted freedom from the problems in my life. It's funny – even years after I surrendered that area of my life to Christ, I have had dreams every now and then about being around horses. When I got around those animals in my dream I tended to forget all about God, and focus all my energy on the horse. That told me that the hold horses held on my life was stronger than I knew.

I believe anything in a person's life could be viewed as an idol if its place is more important in life than commitment to Christ, or commitment to His church. It could be a sport, a lifestyle, even your pocketbook. Jesus can't be number one in our lives until we are willing to surrender these areas in our lives that take up so much of our energy. Possibly He will give them back to us allowing us to enjoy them while putting Him first. But if the Lord does end up taking some of these things away, He will assuredly replace them with something better in our lives.

Those early days in the Lord weren't all peaches and cream, though. Sometimes it's hard to break into a set of people when strong friendships have already been formed. The youth group was all high school age and I didn't feel too welcome there being older than they were. The ones older than me were part of the young married group and I was single. What I ended up doing was fellowshipping with older Saints who took me in and were willing to listen to me. I ended up mostly listening to them, though, and learning what I could from them. I literally felt like a disciple sitting at the feet of a learned Saint of Christ. It was the best thing in the world for me. And it helped to prepare me for the struggles that were yet to come out in the world of business.

CHAPTER SIX

So Much to Overcome

I was listening to Christian radio recently and came across a show on learning disabilities. The show said that learning disabilities were not only a challenge for young children but the problems follow into adulthood. It affects the work life and marriages also, bringing a great deal of frustration. They also had a funny story to share. It dealt with a school boy that had been diagnosed with learning disabilities. The family had set up an appointment for the child to meet with counselors to help in his recovery. Well, the evening of the appointment arrived and the boy's father walked in to the appointment. The receptionist just stared at him with a shocked expression. The father started wondering what was wrong and checked himself out to make sure that he was not the object of her shock. The receptionist recovered and asked where the man's son was. Then the father realized that he had forgotten to pick up his son to bring him to the appointment. With great embarrassment, the father went back home again to get his son and bring him back to the appointment. The professionals involved in the treatment of the child began to wonder if the father, too, was learning disabled! The father and son both were able to be treated for learning disabilities, and all lived happily ever after. What people need to realize is that for a person with severe learning difficulties this is a daily occurrence. There is not a day that does not pose incredible challenges.

This is how I found my life in the working environment. Not only did I have learning challenges, I also had over 20 years of memories of being misunderstood, made to feel "slow", made to feel different. The tape recorded messages in my brain from years of learning frustration reminded me daily that I was different and I probably wasn't smart enough for this job anyhow. For people who hire learning disabled employees it is a real challenge to deal with the high margin of error. I held down jobs here and there. They all started great until the margin of error showed up and then everything hit the skids. Every time this happened (maybe 6 months into the job) and it became apparent to my employer that I did have special challenges I had a decision to make. I needed to decide if the job I had was worth working through the chaos that was to come until I really learned it, or if I should find something easier. The times I did go elsewhere and try something else it did go better for a while until the old pattern came back again. Again the margin of error arose and the chaos started. The employer and the other employees misunderstood, and again I had a decision to make.

One good thing is that during the first few years of my life as a Christian I started training in children's ministry.

I knew soon after I had been filled with the Holy Spirit that God wanted me involved with children but it took me a few years to move into that ministry. Kids, as I have said before, can be very brutal. They know when you are sure of yourself and when you are not. They also know if you really know what you believe. And after you are convinced that you do know what you believe, they will challenge that knowledge. But as I did get involved with a group of children, that was the beginning of the healing of my self esteem. The more I found myself with this group of children the more I saw the person God was making me into, and the more I liked that person. I had a great respect for what God was doing in me and the person he was making me into. Even if I messed up out in the business world I was at home and in my element with these kids.

After a few failed attempts at different careers I found myself working in downtown Seattle for the telephone company. I was being trained as a data entry clerk and again, the margin of error came up. By this time I was desperate. I longed to become good at doing **something**. Finally one night the pressure was so great that I prayed to The Lord. Saying "Lord, what's wrong with me? I know that there is something wrong here. Please show me." I am not a person usually given to visions, but The Lord answered that prayer by giving me one. In this vision I saw what the problem was. The information I was actually seeing with my eyes was correct. But somehow as it traveled to my brain, that information was getting scrambled. Then my hands would obey my brain, putting out the scrambled information it was translating to me.

I knew in my heart that I had heard from God. Then I shared this with the people I worked with and they said, "That's right. You have dyslexia." I never knew that it had a name. Well, I went home from work that night very excited. If this thing had a name then it was something that God could take care of. I called my Pastor the next day and explained what had happened to me and the vision God had given me. And I asked if the church would pray for me that Sunday morning. He agreed and they did. I expected things to change right away, instantaneously. But that didn't happen. In my life, The Lord has chosen to do that slow, steady work of healing emotions as he heals the physical and developmental problems. As time went on I did come to find great freedom, and found the career I loved and was good at. I left the phone company shortly after that for a better shift at another organization. Another attempt at a job that wasn't worth going through the chaos of learning. That job didn't last long either. More frustration at the margin of error, and another employer who misunderstood me. That led to about 9 months of unemployment.

During that time I took a few community college courses to brush up on skills and filled out a lot of job applications, and got a lot of rejections. I remember coming up for prayer one Sunday at my church for help in the situation. There was a man there who had a good prophetic ministry who offered to pray for me. After he prayed, God did give him a word for me. God would indeed help me find the right job, that I would work there for a very long time, and that I would become very good at what I did. My first thought when hearing that word from The Lord was "No Way! That doesn't sound like me." Just a few months after this incident I interviewed for a job at a Christian University in Seattle. I was told that there were actually two jobs available, one for cashiering and one for data entry. Well, I'd done data entry before and didn't really desire to go there again. Another fiasco. I would never even be interested in doing that again. But I felt like I could do the cashiering. So I interviewed for that job. Another girl interviewed on the same day for the data entry position. Well, apparently after the interviews the Controller at this University felt like this other girl would do better for cashiering, and since I had done data entry before he offered me that job. I accepted, and I also learned never to say never again.

Again, the challenge of a new job, and again the margin of error was there. But the Lord was starting to work with me, showing me how to compensate in different situations for the weaknesses. I know that I frustrated most of the people who trained me and that I was frustrated myself by the slow rate I was learning. I put together a good set of job instructions and referred to them over and over. The work situation was such that after the training period I was left alone to work out my own problems and to find the angle that I could learn best from. At normal rate of learning it takes one to two years to learn a job and get really proficient at it. Give a person with learning disabilities five years and they will probably get the job down pretty good. And magnify the frustration level of the employer about ten times and you will start to imagine the frustration level of the poor person who is actually doing the learning. But after the first few years I did learn the job, and yes, I did get very good at it. By the end of my seventh year at the University the people who had seen me struggle to learn the job had all moved on. When I tried to share with people the challenges I have at learning and retaining information nobody believed me! What a change of situation! I'm so glad that I decided that this job was worth going through the chaos of learning, feeling the frustration of others, and of myself also. I also gained a wonderful group of co-workers who loved me and were pulling for me.

CHAPTER SEVEN

Lessons to be Learnied

With the pressure off at work, I could pursue my heart's desire at the church – the children's ministry. By this time I was working full board in the Children's Church, teaching every Sunday morning while the adults were in the morning service. I had a children's drama group and led a children's choir, putting on musicals at Christmas. I also worked with the kids club on Wednesday evening at our church, working with older, pre-teen girls. I felt if God could get them somewhat grounded in the Lord while they were still young and give them a sense that He really did understand them and loved them, that they might have some chance of surviving the teen years. I guess what I really wanted to do was to give back to the next generation what I had so desperately needed growing up, and had not been available to me. I'm not saying that being a Christian would have changed my situation, but it would have changed me. And I know that I would have handled so much better all that happened to me. My desire was to see these kids grow up to be mature, Christian young adults who wanted to be used by God. So far, most of these young people have not let me down, and I am so very proud of the young adults they are becoming.

One year I sponsored a group of Junior High aged girls in our Missionettes club, held on Wednesday nights. This was a very energetic group of girls and they made the class fun and challenging. One evening the class subject somehow got around to physical and sexual abuse. As the conversation progressed I came to find out that 3 out of the 5 girls in the class had been abused and were going through recovery of some type. My heart really went out to them and I encouraged them with the evidence of healing that Christ had already done in my life. Another Wednesday night I showed up with a chalkboard, chalk and an eraser. I divided the chalkboard in half, on one side I wrote all the different issues I dealt with growing up. On the other side of the chalkboard I wrote one or two words for each issue that led to the subject of healing for me. As I expounded on the healing for each issue, I took the eraser and erased the cause of the pain. It was quite an emotional evening for all of us. Another Wednesday night I showed up at class with a bouquet of lovely tulips, not quite opened yet. I was interested in dealing with the "guys" issue, and encouraged them to stay as innocent as possible for as long as possible. These girls had already been exposed to quite a bit, and they had a choice to make – what to do with what they had already been exposed to. I gave each girl a tulip to examine. Then as I got into my lesson, I took one of the petals of the flowers and played with it. "Now, what would happen to this flower if I were to grab one of these petals and pull at it, trying to open the flower before it's time?" The Girls thought for a minute and then they agreed that in doing so I would destroy the flower. I said, "That's right. This flower is not quite open yet. It's not ready. It will open by itself when it's the proper time. Anyone that is encouraging you to do things you know are wrong, or that you aren't comfortable with is taking one of these beautiful petals and pulling at it, trying to open up the flower before it's ready. You need to think about who your friends are and what they are into. Are they safe people to be around or are they into dangerous stuff? If they are, they will be trying to get you into it too. I don't want your life ruined like these flowers would be. When hurtful things happen to you it takes a long time to heal. It would be better to stay out of those situations, or those groups of friends that would bring trouble to you." Needless to say there were hugs all around when the class was over.

I was also coming into my own musically at the church. Years of being faithful in the church choir was paying off and I was really having fun with it. I guess I had a tough lesson to learn about musical talent. The hard lesson was that God Himself is the giver of all talent and that which He chooses to give He can also choose to take away. Growing up, music was the only thing I had going for me. I did get a little of my popularity from sharing it and that bred an attitude in my heart that wasn't the best. In stripping of the attitude, I lost God's blessing on my music and I lost my desire to play and sing. There was a period of three to four years that I didn't touch my instrument and didn't sing at all except for in the church choir. No solos, and no interest to sing one. One way that God used to strip me of my attitude was to place me in the middle of a lot of talented people. When I looked at what they could do and where I was at, I knew I fell very short, In time, God did renew my desire to share musically with a new, more mature attitude – one that sincerely wanted to worship the Lord with my music, not just show off what raw talent I did have.

I believe that the Lord is the creator of real music, and He desires His people to dedicate their talents and abilities to Him. God can truly use a willing heart that sincerely wants to touch others through their musical interest. He can take a very raw talent and bless and anoint it, and cause it to grow far beyond its natural ability. That's what I feel He did with me. I felt impressed right away after the Commitment to Christ to dedicate that musical talent to Him, and that He would take it, increase it, and use it. I encourage you, whatever it is, to commit your talents and abilities to The Lord. If you are into sports, commit that talent and ability to Christ. Put Him first in it and don't let the sport or talent keep you away from your church, or from growth in Christ. Use it in your church instead when you can. God can take that level of commitment far,

In my thirties, life was a whirlwind of activity between career, friends, church, the children's ministry and music. I literally loved every minute. The Lord was also doing a great healing in my spirit during this time from the fear and anxiety that the physical problems as a child had caused. My surgeries left both legs with ugly long scars, and it took years for the post-surgical pain to subside. I would be all right for a while then I would do something that jarred the knee joints and the pain would be intense. I knew there was quite a bit of inflammation that had to be taken care of over time. I remember one experience when I was about 20 years old. I was getting into my car and just happened to hit my knee against the emergency break handle in such a way to actually recreate the pain that I grew up with when my knee dislocated. I must have sat in my car and sobbed for 15 minutes. The trauma was still there in my mind.

I had also come to a place emotionally where I was able to deal with the weight problem and lost 70 pounds. Weight counselors say that every 10 pounds a person loses they must deal with at least one emotional issue that put the weight on in the first place or it won't stay off. The issues that had kept the weight on were finally being dealt with and I was feeling really great. As the weight came off my self-confidence rose to a new level. I could now walk and run without fear. I remember one time I was getting out of my car and my dress moved aside so I could see the scar on one of my knees. I thought, "O Lord, there's those awful scars again." And the Lord spoke to my heart and said, Yes, but the scars inside have been healed. I thought, "That's right!" I had stopped having those mental flashbacks of the knee problem reoccurring, and was feeling more freedom in my life than ever. Thank you Jesus! It took a long time, but I was finally getting somewhere in my quest for healing and wholeness.

Life was perfect. I was enjoying friends, family and church so much. But even in a perfect world, things happen. My best friend had a darling little niece that I was totally in love with. On Memorial Day Weekend of 1987, this little one was hit by a drunk driver, and at the age of 20 months the Lord chose to take her home. That was one of the biggest blows of my life. I couldn't understand why the rest of the world went on, and my world had come to a screeching halt. This was the first tragic death I'd ever dealt with, and it hit hard. I was angry at the world, and at the Lord, but I refused to let that anger take me out of His presence. I went to church, did all the right things, and I knew eventually that God would meet me where I was. I was still very involved with this girls family and I did what I could to help them deal with their loss. But I wasn't dealing at all with my own loss and grief. This led to panic attacks in my mind. With the help of my wonderful Pastor, and the Lord, I did overcome this. It was quite a few years before I stopped dreading Memorial Day Weekend or before I could listen to the song sung at her funeral without going bananas. I know that I will join her some day, when Graduation Day comes my way too.

In time, life was better again. I was deliriously happy. But what it all comes down to is that life is life. And perfect doesn't last forever. What I didn't know was that God was preparing me for the greatest challenge of my life and that He would be there every step along the way, to walk me through each challenge.

CHAPTER EIGHT

Transition

If I had my way I would have stayed in my data entry job for the rest of my life. It had become like a familiar old friend and I was very much in my comfort zone. It consisted of data entry support for the Controllers Office, Accounts Payable, Budget, and General Ledger. I also organized the data entry workload for the month end closes and year end close proceedings. The other part of my data entry job consisted of support to the Business Office which was the Accounts Receivable side of the University. Any tuition payment that came in from a student was written up on a receipt, which was then forwarded to my desk for data entry. During the beginning parts of each quarter, and at statement times, the receipts were quite heavy. I also organized binding and filing of the student account receipts. Financial aid payments were computer generated and it was also part of my duties to enter these into the Accounts Receivable system as well. The Accounts Receivable portion of my job took about half my time, keeping my afternoons busy.

I had spent twelve years at the University and by this time had pretty much worked through the learning disability, making a quality control circle around every project I did to ensure I had caught all my errors. From there, all my work was proofread for corrections. It was a perfect situation for someone with my challenges.

Into the 12th year of my job, the University decided to bring in a new computer program to take care of the Accounts Receivable receipts, entering them into the computer at the time of transaction. During the following year as plans were finalized and the computer program brought in for testing, I began to wonder what would become of my perfect job. Occasionally I would bring the subject up with my bosses, but they were not worried. They liked me and assured me that my job was secure. They still couldn't tell me what I'd be doing though. Finally, in 1992 the new computer program was brought on-line and I was left wondering what would happen to me, where I would end up. The rest of my data entry position took me four hours or less each day, and for the rest of the day I wandered around from desk to desk looking for work. This didn't do a whole lot to boost my self esteem. It was the beginning of a time of trying in my life that led to deep depression. Just when I thought I had a basic idea of what to do with those extra four hours the plans were changed and I was left again without much to do. My supervisors did their best to encourage me, to tell me again that my job was very secure, but there were no answers to where I would eventually end up.

As job openings appeared in my Department I talked to the right people and voiced my interest. I was interviewed for some of them but not chosen. The University's job was to find the best suited person for each opening and that is what they did. Apparently they couldn't see me really shine in those jobs. My talents and abilities were needed elsewhere. I just didn't know where yet. I had no idea how much I had built my self esteem around what I did. It had almost become who I was. That's a very easy pit to fall into. The only problem with that is when the job situation changes, or layoffs come, it's more than the job that will suffer. Over and over again I felt the Lord check my heart – what I did at work wasn't as important to him as who I was in Him. That was such a tough year. I helped in many different areas, learned a lot, but it never lasted very long. Security was not a big word in my life. One thing I have learned about learning disabilities is that they are very much connected to self confidence. When self confidence is lower, the problem gets worse. When it is higher, the "I can do this job" belief comes back strong and you can plough through the confusion.

One of my bosses during this time was so very supportive. She taught me how to do queries, or "selects" on the computer database where you can get pertinent answers from the computer with just a little information. It took me a while to get the hang of doing this but she encouraged me to keep trying. Eventually I did get the hang of it, and it is the procedure I used the most in my next job. About nine months into this transition enrollment took a sudden drop and the University budget hit the skids. There was a report of many job cuts coming. As a matter of fact, 2 or 3 jobs were cut in my Department. But not mine. I was told later that the reason I was kept on staff, even though my workload was not a full 8 hours, was because my bosses liked me and valued me as an employee. They knew I was a very hard worker. I am so thankful that I was surrounded by so much support, and so many people who believed in me. My boss suggested that I take some accounting courses at the Community College and learn more about what the rest of my department did. In the Spring of 1993 I registered for a bookkeeping course at the Community College. I felt like this was something I could handle. Nothing much was happening with the job anyway – yet.

In the middle of July, 1993, it was finally time to pursue more education. It was then I was told that a decision had been made about my job. The supervisor in our Accounts Payable department was retiring after 23 years of service to the University. There would be some duty shifting in that area which left an opening for me to move into Accounts Payable on August 1st. I said "Ok" but mentally and emotionally I was in shock. I had worked enough around Accounts Payable to see the intense detail in that department – and me with my learning handicap. Any time I saw a job opening where the qualifications were "attention to detail" I never applied. But our Director of Finance assured me that this would be the best place for me to compliment my talents and abilities. I figured that God had brought me this far, helping me to learn a new job, and helped me survive a major departmental cut during job transition. I knew I would need His help to survive this! And that very evening I was to begin my first evening of night school. I thought "How did I get myself into this." But I just put one foot in front of the other and kept moving ahead.

I remember the last day of July that year as a day of great sorrow. I truly loved this Accounts Payable supervisor who was retiring. She had very much become a "mom" to the young girls she worked with and I knew I would really miss her. I spent the day cleaning out my office and preparing to occupy my new position. That felt really strange. The Accounts Payable and Payroll Departments posed for pictures to remember her and I joined the group as the rookie A/P person, teary eyes and all. There was one bright moment of that day when some friends around the campus showed up for a surprise good-bye party. They had our catering agency make a cake for the party that was decorated as a request for payment. It was pretty funny. Good byes said, boxes packed, it was time to move across the room to my new job. And frankly, I knew the challenge ahead of me, and that my mind did not naturally work along the lines which the job required. I was scared to death. The question of the day was "what am I doing here?" And I continued to ask myself that question for a long time.

CHAPTER NINE

Life in Accounts Payable

Basically, the Accounts Payable or Payments department pays the bills for our Organization. We view requests for payment, which are submitted to our Department and "account check" them for accuracy. Just to give you an idea of the detail involved in this "account check" here is the routine:

Locate the area on the invoice that states who the check should be made payable to, and make sure that the Departments have made it payable to the correct person or organization.

Find the "remit to" address that appears on the invoice. If there is no "remit to" address choose the address on the invoice and make sure the Department has properly written it under the "remit to" name.

If the vendor is located outside the State of Washington, make sure that they have charged sales tax on the invoice. If they did not, check to see if it is a taxable expense. If it is, you need to charge the Department "use tax" to the tax rate amount of the invoice so that the tax can be paid by the University at the end of the month.

Make sure that the proper invoice number appears in the description column of the Request for Payment.

Locate the invoice date on the invoice and make sure that it has been copied properly onto the Request for Payment.

Locate payment terms on the invoice, and make sure that the due date on the request has been properly assigned for data entry. Checks are pulled by computer according to due date. If there are no terms of payment on the invoice assign the due date 30 days from the invoice date. Make sure that there is not a discount available for quick payment. If there is, adjust the due date and subtract the discount from the amount being paid on the request.

Check to see if the Department has marked if the check is to be picked up or mailed out. If they have marked to be picked up, there is a "pick up" stamp which needs to be firmly stamped by the name and address on the request. If the stamp is not seen and a check is mailed out by accident the Department could be left in a difficult situation.

Make sure that you are paying from an original invoice to keep from double paying. If a photocopy or faxed invoice has been submitted with the request, research to make sure that it has not already been paid, call the Department if necessary to ask if they have an original invoice for this request in their office.

Check the invoice amount, and make sure that the Department has written it properly.

Check Department account numbers to make sure that the proper Department is signing for the request, and that the expense is being properly accounted for.

Check the signatures on the request to make sure that the person signing has signature authority for the department, and for the amount of the expense.

Bring all totals down to the bottom of the request, and make sure it balances.

Make sure that there is a proper business purpose for the request.

This is the procedure for each request for payment. It's enough to make your head spin, right? And there were hundreds of requests going through our Accounts Payable each week. Now you can

understand why it seemed to be an impossible
challenge for me – the naturally dyslexic one.

Because of the change to the old position, there
was a big question as to whether to hire a new person
outside the company to take on the job I had vacated.
The arrangement was that for the first year I would keep
doing the data entry that was left of the old job, and take
on two of the larger account Departments on the Campus
to get my feet wet in Accounts Payable. It was difficult to
get it all done. The data entry end ended up taking me
over 4 hours each day, and being a slower learner it was
hard for me to get the workload done for the new position
in the time allotted. There was also an adjustment from
having my own quiet office which led to an atmosphere
of self confidence for me, to being in very close quarters
with four other people, all who were trying to help me
learn. I was trying desperately to learn, but self confidence
was getting lower all the time. The biggest challenge of
all is that our University is audited yearly due to Federal
requirements, and there was a real need for accuracy in
the work that came across my desk. If the auditors caught
some big errors, it would lead to some big fines. My
University had a very clean audit for years and nobody
wanted that to change. I didn't blame them.

I also felt strongly that even with the pressure and
unhappiness, God had placed me where I was. I remember
the first University communion service we had after the
job change. Something the entire University community
gathers for every September, is to be thankful to God
for the upcoming year, to take communion together and

to receive the State of the University Address from the University President. I remember the President reminding us that we were all there by divine providence, that we were God's choice for what we were endeavoring to do, and reminding us of the mission of the University. That reminder hit me very hard. One year earlier I had no doubt that God had chosen me for what I was doing. Now I wasn't so sure and I wasn't sure that I wanted to continue where I was. The pressure on me was so great. I really wasn't sure I was cut out for this job, that my brain could actually think along the lines that it needed to, to accomplish the task. I also wondered if my Department would be better off with someone who didn't have my learning challenges.

Looking back, it's a very interesting history with that Department. In my time at the University there had been many people in and out and the burnout level was high. I remember people staying in their jobs for maybe 2 or 3 years and then they moved on. I really didn't want to end up that way. I had spent so many good years at the University I didn't want to quit in a down time. If I were to move on, I wanted to really succeed at what I was doing first. Otherwise that would be giving up, just quitting, and I'm not a quitter. It's not that I didn't look around at other jobs either. Part of me longed to find another firm where I could go and do what I was really good at, the data entry end of things. But each time I prayed, and said "Lord, if this is not in your plans, I don't want it". And each time He shut the door.

The depression was getting worse all the time. With the stress of work and night classes I was starting to put on the weight again which I had previously lost. I was continuing with my education, trying to take some Accounting classes at the University. My experience with Financial Accounting was not real successful, but I did pass the course. (Praise the Lord!) My experience with Managerial Accounting didn't go much better. My instructor knew that I was really struggling. In a conversation with him I explained about my learning challenges. He understood. He said "Walking into this course with your learning challenges will not be easy. You will have to study 4 or 5 times longer than the normal student." I knew this already. I remember studying the Accounting problems over and over again and I just couldn't get it. I spent time with my Parents asking them to help. Nearing the end of the quarter I knew that my score was near failure. I asked for prayer at my Church and an interesting thing happened. The weekend before the final test I actually dreamed about those Accounting problems and in my dream I could understand them. When I woke up I still had a good understanding of how to work them. I took that final and aced it, passing the course! The next course I wanted to sign up for, Statistics, needed a basic math completion test. You guessed it, I flunked! I spent that next summer going through basic math skills and learning compensating skills to pass that course. In time I did. I then decided that I'd had enough of higher education for a while.

I remember lifting weights at my health club after work one evening, one way I relieved stress. It was getting so that people I didn't even know were starting to notice that I was depressed. I remember people sort of staring at me and thinking "I wonder what's wrong". As I was using one of the machines I was mulling over the job situation and the challenges I was having and my frustration with myself for not catching on to things faster. I could feel the frustration coming from others around me so strong. I was giving it my best shot and again, I just wasn't measuring up to code. I remember a thought going through my head about the learning disability, like "this is such a curse on my life". And as the thought passed my mind, a light went on in my head. Maybe there was a spiritual side to this problem as well as a physical side. The first thing I did was to get very angry at the problem, and at the enemy of our souls. The second thing I did was to start praying against the influence he had in my life and take authority over this problem in the name of Jesus Christ. I believe a born again child of God who knows their position in Christ can take control of the forces in their life that are holding them back from being their very best for God, and for their organizations. So I just reminded the enemy of who he was, where he was headed, and that Jesus had already won this battle. I started finding some relief then, and that encouraged me to keep praying against the problem. I could actually feel a difference when the disability was really affecting my brain. It felt like something was squeezing the base of my skull like a vice and that it was squeezing my brain too, not allowing me to think straight. When I prayed against the problem it lifted and I could actually think clearer. I also remember God speaking to my heart loud and clear at that moment. I will never forget what he said. He said "If you will walk through this with me one more time, you will never have to deal with this again". I took Him at his word and that gave me courage and confidence to go on.

After that first year, there were more changes at the University concerning my job. The University's Bookstore, my largest account, was sold to another company and the Controller decided it would be a good idea to open my previous position again and allow me to choose to go back to what I was doing or to stay where I was at with a few changes. Part of me longed to go back to familiar territory while the other side of me refused to quit after I had put one year into what I was doing. I felt like it would be taking a step backward. My new position was a slight promotion in pay, and going back to the old job would be going back to the old salary. One of the changes to the new position was to move me to the customer service counter for Accounts Payable and Payroll, allowing me to hand out paychecks to Students and reimbursement checks to Staff. We paid from 600 to 675 students every other week at that time. This would give me a lot more exposure to the students and to others, helping me build strong relationships with people. Part of me jumped at the chance. It really sounded fun. So my decision was made to stay where I was with the changes.

Now it was newer, greater challenges. I had never done any customer service work before. And to begin with I wasn't very good at it. My self confidence was already not the strongest at this point and dealing with aggressive customers didn't help matters any. I was encouraged to get some training in customer service. I learned to write answers to questions on 3 X 5 cards (so I wouldn't forget the answers, right?) One of the cards I wrote said "Life is a stage"! My training taught me that even though I wasn't confident yet in my answers I could act like I was. I was already a pretty decent actress and this gave me a little more confidence. I could play the most self confident person in the world! I still referred to those cards every now and then for many years as a refresher. And by the way, the customer service aspect of my job became my strongest suit and where I really ended up excelling.

CHAPTER TEN

So, Talking About Customer Service

So, how can a naturally dyslexic person make long distance phone calls to Vendors around the country and dial the right number? How can she read invoice numbers or customer numbers that are anywhere from 7 to 20 characters long and get them correct? The Lord did give me some wisdom (tricks) dealing with this. I learned that when I looked at an invoice I really couldn't see the whole picture. But if I were to take a pen or pencil, and pinpoint different parts of the information I could actually focus on that one part of the information. When calling a Vendor, if I took a pen or pencil and followed each digit or letter as I read to them, slowly and concisely, I could actually read it correctly. And the Vendor would actually think that I was self confident by the tone of my voice and by my deliberately saying each number very concisely. What the Vendor didn't know was that this was the only way to read them the number, and get it right. I still use this trick today when I'm making one of those Vendor phone calls.

Now, how can a naturally dyslexic person reach into a paycheck box with 600 student paychecks and pick out the right check for the right student? Many times at first I didn't! It was a constant source of embarrassment and my constant payroll nightmare. One thing I found was that if I took a few seconds and really focused on what I was looking at, many times that information would unscramble. I had to learn to deliberately look at each check I handed out.

Another part of the job was routing Accounts Payable mail, mostly invoices, to Departments responsible for paying them. This took me a little while to get the hang of, but I'd been around long enough to know who people were and where they worked on Campus. But it was hard for me to remember which invoices had gone out from week to week. If a Department or a Vendor called and asked if I had seen an invoice or where I had sent it I would be clueless. With a slight computer upgrade I had an idea. I had access to a basic Excel spreadsheet and I started to enter the invoices and pertinent information into the spreadsheet I created so I could track what had come in and where it was sent. Doing this I also had a tool to tell which invoices were being paid and which ones weren't. It was my responsibility to make sure that past due invoices were sent to the Department as soon as possible and I created a notebook to keep track of them, and also created a separate spreadsheet for the past due invoices. This is another area where I ended up excelling over time. Even though it was difficult sometimes I learned to treat every creditor who called with respect and many times ended up making a friend, asking for a faxed copy of the invoice, and that I would send the Department a reminder. The times I prayed and asked Lord, why am I having to deal with these creditors, his answer was always "Because you have become very good at it."

I think my biggest challenge with the customer service side of my job was that I was very aware that the learning disability affected the way I communicated. I would have the words right in my mind, but when I spoke the words would change. It would change the entire meaning of what I was trying to say. Then I would have to correct what I just said. It was humiliating, especially when I was talking to someone who was on the intimidating side. The only way to handle this problem was with a sense of humor. No matter who I was talking to, I had to learn to laugh at myself. It took a lot of pressure and frustration off. I even learned how to make little jokes about it and make others more at ease about it.

Then, after a few more years, transition hit again. Our Business Office and the Controllers Office had always worked closely together sharing the same office space. Well, the Business Office was moved under another Department and plans were made for the Controller's office to move to a newly remodeled space. The remodel took nearly a year. During that time I heard possibilities of being more of a receptionist in our new office. I knew that there was a lot of effort going into the offices and that they would be very nice. Finally when it was all over we were given a tour of the new facility. It, indeed, was very nice. And I remember the feeling of shock when I realized that I was actually going to be the floor receptionist and when I saw how beautiful the spot was prepared for me, I was overwhelmed. I remember one of my co-workers saying "This is a thank you for all your hard work." I just wanted to cry. It was so beautiful I couldn't believe it was actually mine. And again, I was being placed in a spot without close supervision, away from pressure and with the customers I had learned to love. This was the atmosphere that helped me really learn. But, this story would not be complete without transition hitting one more time.

The person hired to take the old job ended up traveling to Japan for a year to work in an orphanage. Management didn't really have a plan for the position so for a time temporary workers came to fill in the gap. Eventually I was offered the old data entry position back and accepted it. With the new work load the account checking of the request for payments was much reduced, down to one or two departments and much easier.. It seemed like transition had hit full circle. And I was no longer being tailored to fit the job, but the job had now been tailored for me!

Not that things were all peaches and cream after the move. Even though I loved my new working environment the frustration continued. My last few yearly reviews had not gone very well and I didn't blame the management team for their frustration. I knew that I needed to learn faster and that I should have had the job down by now. But I also knew how far I had come. I guess it just wasn't far enough yet. I was desperate for more answers. I knew that one area where I always fell apart was the approval of the request for payments. It was just more detail than my brain could handle. And I still needed to function in that area when my Supervisor was on vacation or overloaded with work. I ended up making a detailed list of instructions and having them by my side every time I had a stack of requests to go over. That helped me some. It was also very difficult for me to manage the detailed paperwork and the multitude of interruptions you can get as a receptionist. The two just didn't seem to go together for me. It was a real lesson in personal strength to keep the "act" going when things inside were turning upside down. When you're the receptionist there is no where to hide, there's no where to go until you can deal with life again. All I could do is turn all the "junk" over to the Lord, which is what I really should have been doing all along. I learned that Jesus died not only for my sins, but for my pain, and for the stresses of life. When I can't handle it any more He always can.

CHAPTER ELEVEN

Vision Therapy

It's interesting sometimes how God moves in our lives, and puts people in our path who can change our lives when we really need them. It truly is divine providence. I was on my way to Portland, Oregon with a group of friends, and had done some sharing with these people about my struggles on the job trying to overcome learning challenges in my technical position. A woman in this group named June had a son who had been struggling with learning as well. Her son had found freedom and healing through vision therapy. Well, June started asking me some questions on the way to Portland about the challenges I was facing and then she shared what had happened with her son. She did some quick exercises with me to check how my eyes tracked together, and then gave me the contact information for her son's eye therapy doctor, and the clinic her son had been to in Lynnwood, Washington. She really encouraged me to call their office and make an appointment for an eye exam. At first I was reluctant. I had been to eye doctors since I was age 10 for checkups and eye glasses and none of them had mentioned a word about this thing called vision therapy. But she explained that many eye doctors are not well trained in vision therapy and sometimes don't know what to look for. It takes a specialist who has specific equipment, and knows how to do special testing. She explained some of her son's challenges. One of the eye problems he was suffering from was that his eyes were not tracking together properly or smoothly. When she moved a pencil in a circular motion in front of him, his eyes could not follow the pencil without jumping. Another problem was that his eyes were "falling asleep" or becoming inactive. I decided that I really had nothing to lose from giving this eye doctor a call. My friend was so excited about what this eye doctor had done for her son and sharing it with me. Maybe there was something to this.

In February of 1997 I had my first appointment. I liked this vision therapist from the instant I met her. I felt a real sisterly bond with her as she is also a Christian woman. She put me through a battery of vision tests that I had never experienced before. In the middle of these tests she stopped and commented to me "I can tell that you are really concentrating on this. It's like you're having to focus completely to get every answer correct. What is it you do for a living?" When I explained my highly technical job to her she was shocked. She said "I really don't know how you can do that job with your challenges. This is amazing." All I could answer her was that God has truly helped me to learn it and to survive it. The diagnosis was quite common for a person with learning challenges. I had the same problem of my eyes not tracking together properly, and not being able to follow an object without jumping. I found out that instead of one eye falling asleep on me, that my eyes alternated. One would fall asleep while the other was still active. And then that eye would turn off while the other eye became active. Another interesting thing they found out during testing was that my eyes were not pointing right. The right eye was fine, pointing straight ahead. The left eye, however, veered off to the left. This created a large "blind spot" where I was missing all this information. That explained so much. Why for most of my life I had been running into things like walls and doorways – I honestly didn't see them properly. Why I had severe depth perception problems when I drove. Why objects seemed closer to me than they actually were. I learned that when I reached for something that was on the table right in front of me my hand would actually miss the object and unconsciously my hand would move over a fraction of an inch to where the object really was. And I didn't even realize I was doing this. She scheduled me right away for appointments with a vision therapist. Normally, vision therapy takes right around six months with weekly visits and daily eye exercises. But in my case the therapy appointments were not covered by my insurance. At seventy dollars a session I could only afford to go in once a month. So that meant I had to work a whole lot harder on my own, doing exercises regularly. I had already become the queen of physical therapy, taking care of joint issues as my body aged and was committed to my home therapy to stay mobile. This was just more to add to that routine. I was determined and motivated. I felt like this was a real Godsend for me in my life and this was His answer to start turning this disability around. With my daily exercises and monthly visits to the therapist office the entire process took about a year and a half.

At that time I had this sweet little (emphasis on the word little) penthouse apartment right across the street from the University campus – all windows with a great view of that area of Seattle, the I-5 freeway heading towards downtown, and the Cascade Mountain Range. This was such a refuge for me, especially in the early morning when I got up to do my therapy routine for my physical issues and watched the sun rise. I went home for lunch every day and worked hard on my vision therapy exercises for an hour before returning back to work – unless I had a work buddy who wanted to come home with me and enjoy some lunch, the view and some chocolate. At that time the office building my parents owned and managed had a tenant where one of the items they sold was specialty chocolate. They were always getting chocolate from this tenant that was not moving fast enough out of their suite, and many times I was the happy recipient. Way to Go! See, things weren't all bad!

So in March, 1997 I began the routine, doing exercises daily during my lunch hour and visiting the vision therapy clinic once a month for evaluation by the trained therapists and to obtain new exercises. The first step was to build a strong foundation for each eye. This was done by wearing a patch over one eye, and doing simple tracking exercises such as following a pencil back and forth, right and left, and in a circular motion. Then I would move the eye patch to the other eye and do the same exercises. Also I put vision charts up on my wall and picked out specific detail on the chart in a specific order or rotation. It was a lot of hard work and was sometimes very discouraging. The problems at work were still very much on my mind and I guess I was looking for immediate results. I remember the mornings when I would pray "Please work with these eye exercises to make permanent changes in the way I see things. Please help me interpret information the way it actually appears. And please help me to communicate information properly." It seemed like that goal was so far away. But I continued to work at it.

Over time I could move away from using the eye patch so much, and it was time to start working both eyes together and working on tracking more. The foundation of each eye had been strengthened to a point that the eye patch was no longer necessary. Instead I started using word search books and word & picture mazes, working on picking out detail. Flip-lenses and prisms took the place of the eye patch. Even at the first six months I really didn't see much change yet, but when I went in for my therapy appointments the vision therapists were starting to literally bounce off the walls with excitement. They could see the progress that I couldn't see. I guess I was looking for a lightning bolt kind of change where suddenly everything was clear and easy. That is not part of the game. What happens is small changes over time, and then one day you wake up to find that changes are really taking place. This started one Sunday morning in Church as I was dutifully taking sermon notes. I looked down at the notebook I was writing in to realize that my handwriting was changing. I busily thumbed through my notebook to see the beginning entries that I had written months earlier, and sure enough. My letters were becoming a consistent size. This was one thing I had always struggled with before – writing letters and numbers to the same proportion of size. I just couldn't do it no matter how hard I tried. But this was starting to change. Right now I am proud to say that my penmanship is so much improved that sometimes I can't even believe that it's my writing. Recently I started working for my parents part time on the weekends to help with paperwork in the office building they own and manage. My mother is always commenting on my improved handwriting! But this is only the beginning!

The next thing I noticed was that reading was becoming much easier. Even though I still pick up a pencil and follow each character when communicating invoice numbers over the phone at work, I found I was actually picking out the proper paychecks out of the check box without as much effort. This was a great relief. And it just made me more determined to keep working on the eye exercises, working toward that perfect goal.

I still had a long ways to go. I was looking for a change still in the way I communicate, that the words I intend to say would actually come out the way I intend, and I was also looking forward to the great "mental awakening" that would help me think smarter. I asked my therapist one day if the vision therapy would help my thought process, and she had an interesting analogy to answer my question. Say you are looking through a window that is very dirty and muddy. It's hard to see outside objects clearly isn't it? Well, it's the same way with learning challenges. If there are blockades in the mind that keep you from seeing clearly how can you expect to think clearly? I am so thrilled with the progress I have made and I know that it is changing my life.

I believe that there are no easy answers to why challenges come into our lives. I really have no clue why other people have this kind of eye treatment covered by their medical insurance and are able to find freedom in six months with treatment, while it takes me a year and a half because I can only afford to come into the clinic once a month. I have no idea why I was placed in the job I hold that is beyond my natural abilities. There are no easy answers to why I was faced with the physical challenges and learning difficulties. I had to learn to overcome. One thing I found is that success is so much sweeter when you really have to fight for it, and I guess this is the story of my life. In those moments when I've been so overwhelmed from exhaustion and discouragement I have prayed to the Lord, asking him "Why did you make me this way anyway?" His answer in life has always been the same. "So that you may learn to overcome." The Lord Jesus has taught me how to be a real life overcomer, and you can be one too. Just lean on the Lord, the creator of all things, look for support from friends and family, and like I did, find people at work who believe in you. Be positive about yourself and develop a "I can do this" mentality. With hard work and persistence, powerful changes can come.

CHAPTER TWELVE

The Prayer of Faith

Beginning a relationship with Christ is not a difficult thing to do. It does, however, imply that you see a need for God's help in your life. The Bible says in Romans 3:23 that **all have sinned, and come short of the Glory of God.** Isaiah 53:4-6 says **Surely he took our infirmities and carried our sorrows, yet we considered him stricken by God, smitten by him and afflicted. But he was pierced for our transgressions, he was crushed for our iniquities; the punishment that brought us peace was laid on him and by his wounds we are healed. We all, like sheep, have gone stray, each of us has turned to his own way; and the Lord has laid on him the iniquity of us all.** And then the passage goes on to describe the suffering of Christ on the cross. He truly died not only to save our souls, but also to give us the strength and power to overcome in this life. Many people are discouraged from making a commitment to the Lord in their lives thinking "I'll never make it. I can't change. I won't have any friends, or any more fun in my life. I've made too many mistakes anyway. How can I get rid of all my bad habits? Don't I have to clean up my act before God can accept me?" Absolutely not! Don't even worry about the lifestyle you are living right now. If it is against the Word of God, He will convince you of that and at the same time give you the power to change it. All he requires is that you listen to his voice and act accordingly. Well, here it is. All you need to do is pray this prayer of Salvation – let God in and he will take it from there.

DEAR LORD JESUS, I THANK YOU FOR YOUR HEARING MY PRAYER RIGHT NOW. I ACKNOWLEDGE THAT I AM A SINNER BY NATURE AS ALL HUMAN BEINGS ARE. I THANK YOU FOR DYING ON THE CROSS FOR ME FOR SHEDDING YOUR BLOOD THAT I MIGHT HAVE LIFE. COME INTO MY HEART RIGHT NOW AND MAKE ME CLEAN. WASH AWAY ALL THE WRONG I HAVE DONE, AND MAKE ME NEW. I WANT TO SERVE YOU, AND BE YOUR CHILD. THANK YOU FOR ANSWERING MY PRAYER. IN JESUS NAME, AMEN.

If you have prayed this prayer, it is very important to your future as a Child of God that you find a church in your area to become involved in that preaches the Word of God. God never meant for any of us to be "lone rangers" in our walk with Him. You need the support and friendship of others who have also prayed the same prayer you have. If the church you find is a large one, try to find a small home group or bible study so that you can create strong bonds with others in the faith. And let God help you in those areas of your life that are destructive and need to change. He is so faithful to encourage us in those areas and will literally give you the power to change and become a better person. I believe that Jesus not only died for our sins, but also for the stresses of life. The foot of His cross in the perfect resting place for those burdens and concerns of this life. The God of the universe is big enough to keep the world from destroying itself, but also small enough to be concerned with each of our daily life's problems. God bless you and keep you on the road to new faith in Him.

Printed in the United States
By Bookmasters